HILLTOP ELEMENTARY SCHOOL

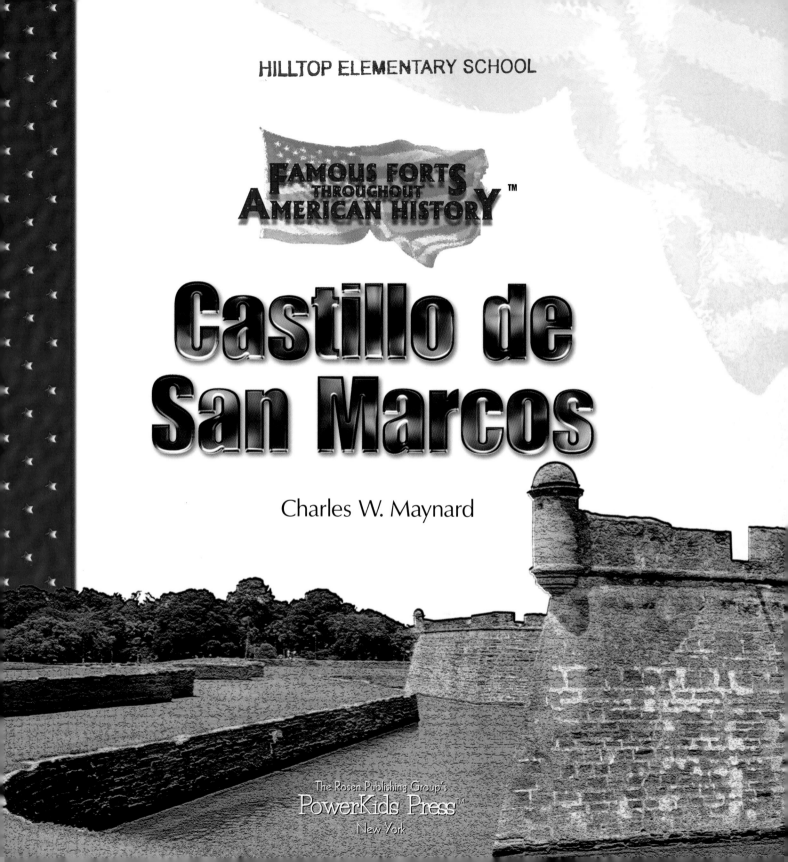

HILLTOP ELEMENTARY SCHOOL

FAMOUS FORTS
THROUGHOUT
AMERICAN HISTORY ™

Castillo de San Marcos

Charles W. Maynard

The Rosen Publishing Group's
PowerKids Press™
New York

For Lou and John, wonderful parents who honeymooned in the shadow of the Castillo

Published in 2002 by The Rosen Publishing Group, Inc.
29 East 21st Street, New York, NY 10010

First Edition

Book Design: Michael Caroleo

Project Editor: Kathy Campbell

Photo Credits: Title page © Karen Huntt H. Mason/CORBIS; pp. 4 (all), 19 (General Marion) © Bettmann/CORBIS; p. 7 © William A. Bake/CORBIS; pp. 8–9 © Dave G. Houser/CORBIS; p. 11 © James L. Amos/CORBIS; p. 12 (Fort Matanzas) © Dorothy Burrows; Eye Ubiquitous/CORBIS; p. 12 (peninsula) © Tim Page/CORBIS; p. 12 (Fort Mose drawing) © Florida Museum of Natural History; pp. 15 (James E. Olgethorpe), 16 (Edward Rutledge), 19 (Native Americans) © CORBIS; p. 15 (corner turret) © Richard Cummins/CORBIS; p. 16 (courtyard) © Raymond Gehman/CORBIS; p. 20 © Reinhard Eisele/CORBIS.

Maynard, Charles W. (Charles William), 1955–
Castillo de San Marcos / Charles W. Maynard.— 1st ed.
   p. cm. — (Famous forts throughout American history)
Includes bibliographical references (p.   ) and index.
ISBN 0-8239-5841-8 (library binding)
1. Castillo de San Marcos (Saint Augustine, Fla.)—History—Juvenile literature. 2. Castillo de San Marcos National Monument (Saint Augustine, Fla.)—Juvenile literature. 3. Fortification—Florida—Saint Augustine Region—History—Juvenile literature.
4. Saint Augustine (Fla.)—Buildings, structures, etc.—Juvenile literature. 5. Saint Augustine (Fla.)—History, Military—Juvenile literature.
6. Spaniards—Florida—Saint Augustine—History—Juvenile literature. [1. Castillo de San Marcos (Saint Augustine, Fla.)] I. Title.
F319.S2 M39 2002
975.9'18—dc21

                                                                                                00-013205

Manufactured in the United States of America

Contents

Top: *The English navigator Sir Francis Drake and 2,000 men burned St. Augustine and battled the Spaniards in 1586.*
Bottom: *This is a plan of the fort that Pedro Menéndez de Avilés built at St. Augustine, Florida, in 1565 and 1566. The plan was drawn from memory in the late sixteenth century.*

St. Augustine and Florida

With flags flying and weapons ready, Spanish soldiers led by Pedro Menéndez de Avilés landed on the shores of Florida in September 1565. Spain had claimed Florida during earlier visits by Spaniards. The French soon settled in Spanish Florida, too. The Spaniards built a small fort to **defend** themselves against an attack by the French, who had built a fort nearby. When the French fleet sailed to the new Spanish settlement, called **St. Augustine**, strong winds and heavy rains hit the ships and wrecked them. The Spaniards **massacred** the French soldiers who had swum ashore. The place where they killed the French was called Matanzas, the Spanish word for massacre.

St. Augustine grew in size and importance. It was a stopping place for Spanish ships traveling from South America and Mexico to Spain. English pirates, such as John Davis, began to attack the settlement. In 1669, Davis's pirates killed 60 people during an attack.

Building the Castillo

The Spaniards tried to protect St. Augustine by building a wooden fort. The fort soon rotted in the wet Florida weather. Another **fortification** replaced it. From 1565 to 1672, nine wooden forts were built near the settlement of St. Augustine.

On October 2, 1672, work began on a stone fort along the shores of the Matanzas River. Large blocks of a stone called coquina (pronounced koh-KEE-nuh) were cut from Anastasia Island. Coquina is stone made of tiny seashells. Laborers carried the large stone blocks across the bay by boat to the site of the new fort.

Spanish craftsmen worked with local Native Americans to build the fort. The 30-foot-high (9.1-m-high) walls were 14 feet (4.3 m) thick at the base and 9 feet (2.7 m) thick at the top. A water-filled moat, or wide ditch, reaching all the way around the fort made it harder to attack. It took from 1672 to 1695 to finish the fort, which the Spaniards named Castillo de San Marcos.

This view of the Castillo de San Marcos shows the southwest corner, the Bastion San Pedro, and the moat. From the gun deck, visitors can look toward the town of St. Augustine.

The northeast corner of the Castillo is where the largest watchtower, Bastion San Carlos, is located. Defenders of the Castillo used this watchtower to look for enemy attacks from Matanzas Bay. The cannons have movable bases so that they can be aimed.

Under Attack

The first attack against Castillo de San Marcos came in November 1702. Governor James Moore of Charles Town, Carolina, led an English force against St. Augustine. As the English army marched toward the town, the people of St. Augustine crowded into the fort for protection. For nearly two months, they stayed inside the fort. The Spaniards fired the Castillo's guns to destroy the buildings in town closest to the fort so the English could not hide in them. The English surrounded the fort and fired their cannons at it. The coquina stone walls did not break when the cannonballs hit them. Instead they **absorbed** the cannonballs. When Spanish ships from Cuba trapped the English ships in the harbor, the English burned their ships and the town of St. Augustine and fled over the land.

Structure of the Castillo

The Castillo was a large square with **bastions** at each corner. One-foot-thick (30.5-cm-thick) wooden beams formed the **terreplein**, or gun deck. A drawbridge led from the **ravelin** to the **sally port**. Three wells in the **Plaza de Armas** provided fresh water for drinking. The Castillo had 20 rooms to house soldiers, a chapel, food, gunpowder, and supplies.

In 1738, and from 1752 to 1756, the Spaniards improved the Castillo. Coquina stone and lime cement replaced the rotting wood of the terreplein. Thick, stone walls inside the fort added strength and protection. Workers covered the outside walls with white **plaster** to keep the inside from getting damp. They painted the tower of each bastion red. The red and white of the Castillo matched the white Spanish flag with its red X, which flew over the fort. They also built walls around St. Augustine.

Castillo de San Marcos means Castle of St. Mark in Spanish. It was named for this saint because the building of the first wooden fort began on St. Mark's Day in April.

1. Bastion San Augustín
2. Ravelin
3. Bastion San Pedro
4. Sally Port
5. Plaza de Armas
6. Bastion San Carlos
7. Moat
8. Bastion San Pablo

Top: *The Spaniards built the coquina stone watchtower of Fort Matanzas to guard against English ships that might try to surprise the Castillo from the south.*

Middle: *The governor of Florida, Manuel Montiano, founded Fort Mose in 1738 to protect former African slaves.*

Bottom: *Fort Matanzas is located on Anastasia Island, the island where the Spaniards cut the coquina stone for building the Castillo de San Marcos.*

Fort Mose and Fort Matanzas

Black slaves who escaped from the English colonies came south to Spanish Florida to live in freedom. Many brought useful skills. Florida's governor, Manuel Montiano, built a fort 2 miles (3.2 km) north of the Castillo in 1738. Gracia Real de Santa Teresa de Mose, or Fort Mose, was the first free black settlement in North America. Fort Mose provided safety, freedom, and land to Africans who had been slaves.

From 1740 to 1742, the Spaniards built Fort Matanzas, a large stone watchtower on an island 14 miles (22.5 km) south of the Castillo at Matanzas Inlet. Wooden watchtowers stood on the same spot for many years. The new coquina stone watchtower served as a guard to the "back door" of Castillo de San Marcos and as a lookout for approaching enemies.

Another Attack

The English established a new colony, called Georgia, north of Spanish Florida. English general James Oglethorpe led a force of 900 men in seven warships to attack St. Augustine in 1740. Fort Mose fell to the English. A small group of Spanish soldiers forced the English soldiers out of Fort Mose, but they could not force them away from St. Augustine.

Oglethorpe and his men surrounded the white-walled Castillo de San Marcos. They **bombarded** the fort for 38 days. One story tells how each night during the battle the Spaniards would repaint the white walls of the Castillo where English cannonballs had struck. In the morning, the English could not tell whether their cannons had damaged the fort.

When Spanish ships came from Cuba, General Oglethorpe loaded his men onto ships and sailed away after their 38-day **siege**. Of the 750 Spanish defenders in the Castillo, only two died.

The Spaniards painted the 30-foot-high (9-m-high) walls of the Castillo each night so the English could not see whether their cannons had damaged them.

In 1740, General James Oglethorpe and his English force of 900 soldiers, sailors, and Native Americans fired on the Castillo from Matanzas Bay.

Top: Edward Rutledge, a signer of the Declaration of Independence, was held prisoner at the Castillo during the American Revolution.

Bottom: The Castillo's courtyard is lined with guard stations and storage rooms. Soldiers lived in St. Augustine and came to the fort for their turn of guard duty.

The English Have the Fort

The English gained control of the Castillo in 1763, without firing a shot. Spain gave up Florida to England in the First **Treaty of Paris**. The English renamed Castillo de San Marcos, calling it Fort St. Mark.

At first the English made few changes to the old fort. Then in 1775, the **American Revolution** began. Fort St. Mark became a center for the English army in the southern colonies in the fight against the colonists. The English improved the fort by repairing the gates and wells and adding rooms for the soldiers. During the war, the fort served as a prison for American patriots. Three signers of the **Declaration of Independence**, Edward Rutledge, Thomas Hayward, and Charles Pinckney, stayed in the prison.

Spain helped the American colonists in their effort to defeat the English. In 1783, at the end of the war, the English returned Florida to Spain through the Second Treaty of Paris. After 21 years, the Spaniards once again returned to Castillo de San Marcos.

Fort Marion

Spain did not keep Florida for long. In 1821, Florida became a part of the United States. The U.S. Army renamed the Castillo. It was called Fort Marion, in honor of a hero of the American Revolution, General Francis Marion, the Swamp Fox. The fort once again became a prison. In the 1830s, the Army made the old stone storerooms into prison cells for Seminoles, Native Americans who lived in Florida and who fought in a war against the Army.

During the **Civil War** (1861–1865), the fort changed hands from the **Union** to the **Confederacy** and then back to the Union, all without a shot being fired. After the Civil War, the Army continued to use the fort

Top Right: *In 1825, the U.S. Army renamed the Castillo, calling it Fort Marion for General Francis Marion, an American hero during the Revolution. Marion was called the Swamp Fox because he attacked English troops and escaped into swamps.*

Bottom: *After the Civil War, the U.S. Army used Fort Marion, as the Castillo was called at that time, as a prison. Native Americans, such as the Comanche, were kept as prisoners at the fort during times of disagreement.*

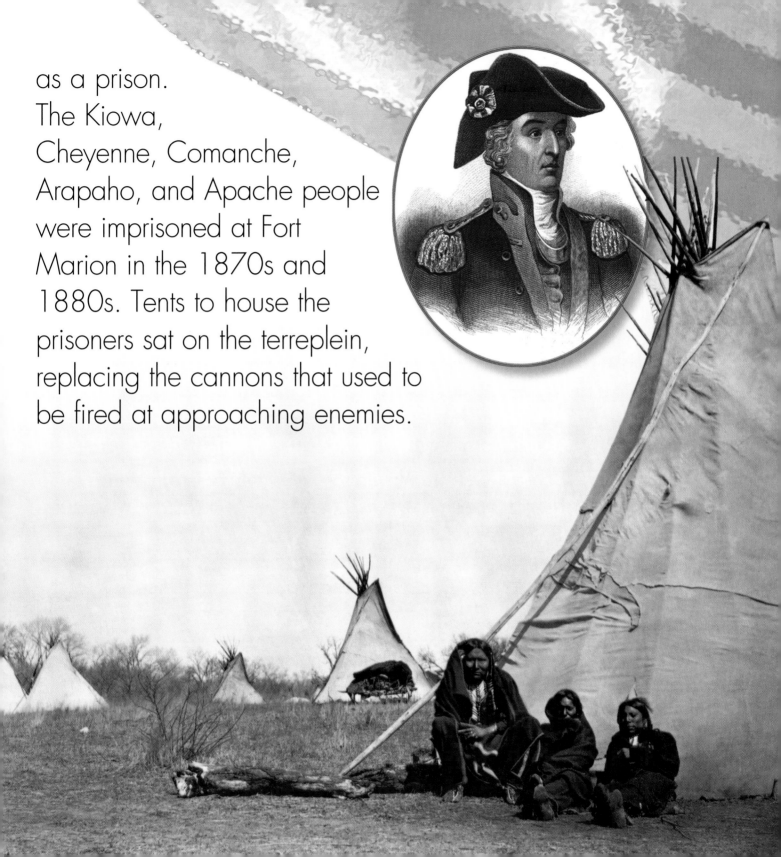

as a prison.
The Kiowa,
Cheyenne, Comanche,
Arapaho, and Apache people
were imprisoned at Fort
Marion in the 1870s and
1880s. Tents to house the
prisoners sat on the terreplein,
replacing the cannons that used to
be fired at approaching enemies.

Timeline

1513 Spanish explorers with Ponce de León land in Florida.

1565 Spaniards establish St. Augustine and fight the French at Fort Caroline.

October 2, 1672 Work on building Castillo de San Marcos is begun.

August 1695 The building of Castillo de San Marcos is completed.

1702 Carolinians burn St. Augustine and the Castillo survives a siege.

1738 The Spanish governor grants freedom to runaway slaves. Black families begin to build Fort Mose.

1740 The English siege is broken with a battle at Fort Mose.

1740-42 Fort Matanzas is built.

1763 Great Britain receives Florida from Spain in the First Treaty of Paris. The Castillo is renamed Fort St. Mark.

1783 The Second Treaty of Paris ends the American Revolution and returns Florida to Spain. Fort St. Mark becomes Castillo de San Marcos again.

1821 Spain gives Florida to the United States.

1825 Castillo de San Marcos is renamed Fort Marion.

1845 Florida becomes a state.

1861-62 Fort Marion is occupied by the Confederacy from January 1861 to March 1862.

1900 Fort Marion is taken off the list of active forts.

1924 The U.S. government declares Fort Marion and Fort Matanzas national monuments.

1933 Fort Marion is transferred from the War Department to the National Park Service.

1942 Fort Marion is once again called Castillo de San Marcos.

Flags over the Castillo

Fort Marion served as a fort and prison from 1695 to 1900 under the flags of four different nations. Even though the fort withstood many attacks, never did the white flag of **surrender** fly over its walls. In 1942, to honor the long Spanish involvement in the fort, Fort Marion was renamed Castillo de San Marcos. Today the Castillo is a national monument to remind us of the Spaniards who first settled North America. The settlement of St. Augustine was established 42 years before the English came to Jamestown, Virginia. Many changes have happened around the old fort that still guards the waters of the bay at St. Augustine.

This cannon sits along the terreplein, which is sometimes called the fighting deck, between Bastion San Carlos and Bastion San Augustín. The cannons located here face the Atlantic Ocean. Guards posted here had a grand view of enemy ships that might try to attack St. Augustine.

Visiting the Castillo Today

Today visitors can cross the drawbridge over the waters of the moat to enter the 300-year-old stone fort. You can stroll by the old cannons on the terreplein and look out at the harbor where Spanish ships carrying gold once anchored. Exhibits and demonstrations show the many stages of the Castillo's history. The National Park Service cares for this oldest masonry fort in the United States.

Near the Castillo, visitors can go to the reconstructed Fort Mose and Fort Caroline. The old lookout station at Fort Matanzas is still standing. The city of St. Augustine, Florida, offers the chance to see buildings and walls in the oldest continually occupied European settlement in the United States. Spain's effect on the early settlement of North America can be seen even today in many old buildings.

Glossary

absorbed (uhb-ZORBD) To have taken in and held onto something.

American Revolution (uh-MER-uh-ken reh-vuh-LOO-shun) The war that American colonists fought from 1775 to 1783 to win independence from England.

bastions (BAS-chunz) Works of earth, brick, or stone that stand out from a fortified work.

bombarded (bom-BARD-ed) Attacked with bombs or big guns.

Civil War (SIH-vul WOR) A war between two sides within one country. A Civil War was fought in the United States between the Union (northern states) and the Confederacy (southern states) between 1861 and 1865.

Confederacy (con-FEH-deh-ruh-see) A group of 11 Southern states, called the Confederate States of America, that tried to leave the United States from 1861 to 1865.

Declaration of Independence (deh-kluh-RAY-shun UV in-duh-PEN-dents) A paper signed on July 4, 1776, declaring that the American colonies were free from English rule.

defend (dih-FEND) To protect someone or something from attack or harm.

fortification (for-tih-fih-KAY-shun) A strong building or place that can be defended against an enemy.

massacred (MA-sih-kurd) To have killed a number of helpless people in a cruel way.

plaster (PLAS-ter) A pasty mixture of lime, sand, and water used for coating walls.

Plaza de Armas (PLA-zuh DUH ARM-us) Spanish for the Place of Arms. It is a large courtyard inside a fort.

ravelin (RAV-lin) A triangular-shaped, stone and earth structure built to protect the entrance to a fort.

sally port (SA-lee PORT) The entrance of a fort, having two sets of large doors.

siege (SEEJ) The surrounding of a fort or town by an enemy who intends to make the inhabitants give up.

St. Augustine (SAYNT AW-gus-teen) A city in Northern Florida named for Saint Augustine because the site was first seen on the saint's feast day in 1565.

surrender (suh-REN-der) To give up.

terreplein (TER-eh-playn) A flat surface on the top of the walls of a fort where guns or cannons are mounted.

Treaty of Paris (TREE-tee UV PAR-es) The name of several important peace agreements signed at or near Paris, France.

Union (YOON-yen) The United States of America, especially during the Civil War.

Index

Web Sites

To learn more about Castillo de San Marcos, check out these Web sites:
www.harcourtschool.com/activity/castillo/castillo.html
www.nps.gov/casa/index.htm